Meditations for Codependents

HAZELDEN

1817

A Harper/Hazelden Book
Harper & Row, Publishers, San Francisco
New York, Grand Rapids, Philadelphia, St. Louis
London, Singapore, Sydney, Tokyo, Toronto

 For information address Harper & Row, Publishers, Inc., 10 East 53rd Street, New York, NY 10022.

FIRST HARPER & ROW EDITION PUBLISHED IN 1989.

Library of Congress Catalog Card Number: 89–45619

ISBN 0-06-255404-2

89 90 91 92 93 SEXTON 10 9 8 7 6 5 4 3 2 1

INTRODUCTION

You will learn to play a starring role in your own life. . . . Now it is time to practice new ways to handle old situations.

—Judi Hollis
from *Fat Is a Family Affair*

When we learn we can't control others' lives, we can turn our attention to our own. We concentrate on our responsibilities and choices. We learn to take care of ourselves physically, mentally, emotionally, and spiritually. We learn to play a starring role in our own lives.

But as Judi Hollis points out, "Most of us are initially scared of starring in our own lives, let alone directing them." We fear what we don't know about. We fear trying something we've never done before. We fear making mistakes and failing. These fears are natural, but they don't have to hinder our progress. We can move through them to new behaviors and healthier, happier lives.

This new way of living calls upon our courage, persistance, and patience. We can learn to set our goals and make our decisions. We can learn to love ourselves, take care of ourselves, believe in ourselves, and accept success and happiness. We can practice being centered in the present moment and accepting the changes in ourselves and our lives. Gradually, our new attitudes and behaviors become part of us. Hand in hand with our Higher Power, we can become the authors, directors, and stars of our lives.

Solitude

As we grow in serenity and self-love, we learn to take care of ourselves by letting go. But, letting go of old relationships, even if they were destructive, can leave us feeling lost and alone.

Someday we may find a new lover and new friends, but until then, our solitude doesn't have to be unhappy. We can love ourselves regardless of other relationships in our lives.

In solitude, we can get to know ourselves better than ever. We can spend time learning and growing and concentrating on our well-being. We can develop ourselves physically, mentally, emotionally, and spiritually. We can focus on our relationship with our Higher Power.

Solitude spent in this way will enrich us and every relationship God has in store for our future.

I will use my time alone, fully, instead of worrying and wishing for relationships.

Miracles

We may have believed the term *miracle* refers only to rare, spectacular, supernatural feats. But life is full of miracles.

The trees, flowers, fruits, and vegetables that grow from tiny seeds are miracles. An act of kindness is a miracle. The peaceful, perfect warmth of love is a miracle. Purring kittens and crying babies are miracles. The rebirth of nature after a long, hard freeze is truly miraculous. We are all miracles.

Several English dictionaries define *miracle* as "an act of God" or "a wonderful thing." Surely all acts of God are wonderful things and all wonderful things are acts of God.

God speaks to us softly, in little things. That's why we must be still and listen.

I see God in everything.

Accepting Our Good

In order to accept new, happy, wonderful events, circumstances, and relationships into our lives, we have to see ourselves as good and deserving. If we accept the good in ourselves, we can accept good things happening for us.

In the past, our negative self-image may have sabotaged our happiness. We could not accept our own good, so we stopped good things from happening to us. Judging ourselves harshly and expecting the worst was part of our old self-defeating way of life. We can now open ourselves up to receiving love, joy, and success by accepting our own worth.

As we move ever forward, we can remember that what we believe about ourselves we will create in our lives. Keeping our focus on our goodness will help goodness flow into our lives.

I deserve to be happy and I am.

Self-Talk

All day long, we silently talk to ourselves. We evaluate situations, make decisions, and constantly monitor our behavior. What do we tell ourselves? What is our attitude and tone? Do we scold or encourage ourselves, or tell ourselves that nothing we do matters anyway?

Self-talk is one of the things we have some control over. We can fill our minds with positive thoughts and images. This can remove the power we may have given to the negative, angry, or belittling voices in our minds.

Talking to ourselves in a kind, gentle, encouraging way can bring out the best in us. Our attitudes and behaviors begin as thoughts. Positive thoughts become positive actions. A loving, affirming pep talk has far better results than a critical, disparaging tirade. There is power in positive self-talk.

I will talk to myself in a loving, encouraging way.

Snail's Pace

In an age of instant foods, automated bank tellers, and express elevators, we may become impatient with things that take time. We may expect love at first sight, overnight success, and quick cures for everything from the common cold to codependency.

Recovery, like life, unfolds in its own time. Good, healthy relationships gradually grow deeper and stronger. Knowledge and maturity evolve a bit each day. Time is our ally. Coupled with our own effort, the passage of time brings incomparable rewards.

We can remember that growth at a snail's pace is still growth. Impatience distracts us from the tiny step we need to take today. If we concentrate on our tiny steps, we will soon find we've covered a great deal of ground. At a snail's pace, we will get where we're going.

I now let go of impatience and concentrate on today.

Self-Love

We may have been confused about self-love in the past. We may have felt selfish and guilty whenever we took care of ourselves. We may not have understood the difference between loving ourselves and being self-absorbed or conceited.

Conceit, egotism, and selfishness are defenses against expected—and in our minds, deserved—attacks. True self-love is the opposite.

Self-love means knowing we deserve to be healthy and whole. It's taking care of ourselves, gently and generously. It's accepting help when we need it from our Higher Power and other people.

We cannot be ready to receive love from others until we embrace ourselves with love. We cannot extend love until we recognize our own goodness. Loving ourselves is healing ourselves.

I love and care for myself.

Detachment

We will always be surrounded by other people and their problems. If we attach ourselves to them, we lose ourselves in the quicksand of codependency. But we can learn to live in this world without sinking into that trap.

We can be kind and caring, and yet keep a healthy distance between ourselves and others. We can listen to others when they need to tell their story, but we don't have to have answers for them. We can let others make their own choices and live with the consequences without trying to save them.

We can do all of this by staying focused on our own inner voice, our Higher Power, our spiritual path. We can avoid the quicksand by walking on the high ground of detachment.

I let go of other people and their problems, with respect for my own inner guide and theirs.

Growing Pains

As recovering codependents, we are practicing letting go of people and circumstances we can't control. This letting go can sometimes be painful. We feel the pain of separation from people who may have been close to us. We feel the pain of change, of facing new and unknown ways of living our lives. We feel the pain of growth.

These experiences stretch us, and teach us about new possibilities. They deepen our understanding and our ability to move on to healthier, more fulfilling relationships. Instead of clinging to our pain, we can move through it and then let it go. We can let it teach us and heal us and strengthen us. We can grow through our pain by accepting its lessons.

I accept that some pain is part of a full life. I try to learn and grow through my pain and then let it go.

Accepting Imperfection

As we walk the path of our lives, we sometimes stumble. Sharp rocks and deep potholes seem to trip us up unexpectedly. Sometimes we fall over our own feet. It is the same for everyone else. None of us are ever perfect.

We can remember that each time we fall, we are learning something, growing in some way. Imperfection is as much a part of being human as breathing. Accepting the ups and downs of life allows us to be open to life's lessons.

We can't feel joyous or achieve perfect success in everything we do. We can learn to accept ourselves and others as imperfect human beings, just trying to do our best. Our Higher Power doesn't expect perfection from us either. All that is asked is that we keep getting back up and taking one more step.

I forgive myself for my imperfection, and accept the constant ebb and flow of life.

Living Spiritually

Many of us may have thought of a spiritual life as one of self-imposed seclusion, austerity, poverty, and celibacy. But while this is one choice for living, it isn't for all, or even most of us. We can live fully enjoying work, recreation, comfort, and various relationships with others, while still maintaining our spirituality.

Only when we become obsessed with the external things in our lives do they impede our spiritual growth. Living spiritually means knowing that everything we need and want — love, peace, joy, serenity, safety, and hope — comes to us from our Higher Power. It means taking time to remind ourselves that we are spiritual, and not just physical beings.

I live my life guided by my spirit and Higher Power.

Accepting Change

Change is as continuous as life. Fighting change is futile. Children grow up, the stock market rises and falls, one season follows another. Change happens, whether we welcome it or not.

In choosing recovery, we are accepting change from day to day and moment to moment. Working our program allows our Higher Power to produce changes in us and our lives. If we let go with grace, each passing moment brings us a little farther along our spiritual path.

As we mature emotionally and spiritually, we see that changes don't have to hurt us. They bring us new experiences, lessons, and insights. They help us grow beyond each passing experience and into the next. Each lesson is important, and the changes in our lives take us through the lessons we need.

My life changes with each passing day. I welcome these changes and the lessons they bring.

Be Here Now

How much time do we waste feeling guilty or angry over the past or worrying about the future? Each moment as it comes can slip away from us when we are lost in such anxious thoughts.

To Be Here Now means to focus fully on each moment as it occurs. The past is gone and the future is but a dream. This very moment, right here and now, is where we have to live our lives.

We can help ourselves concentrate on the present moment. Activities that engage us fully and keep our minds focused make it hard to dwell on our imagined worries. We can play basketball, plant a garden, or paint a room. We can clean out our closets and give the things we no longer use to a charity organization. We can refinish a table, reupholster a chair, or take an exercise class. We can Be Here Now.

I now focus fully on each present moment as it occurs.

Peace of Mind

What could be a greater goal in life than peace of mind? What asset could be of more value to us than unshakable calmness and tranquility? What better evidence of spiritual strength could we have than a peaceful mind and heart?

Peace of mind comes from accepting what we can't control and taking responsibility for what we can. It grows out of faith in our Higher Power and our spiritual natures. It comes to us when we let go of our guilt, fear, and doubt. It is the result of forgiving ourselves and others for all human imperfections.

Without peace of mind, no amount of wealth or good fortune can ever make us truly happy. With true peace of mind, no adversity or lack can ever disturb our calm center.

I let go of guilt, fear, and doubt, and accept the blessing of peace of mind.

Independence

In the past, we may have depended on others for our feelings, opinions, decisions, and self-image. As we have grown and let go of unhealthy dependency, we have learned many new ways of living.

But healthy independence does not mean we have to be totally self-sufficient all the time. In fact, we are all interdependent in many ways. We need farmers, truck drivers, and grocers to get our food. We need the expertise and skill of physicians and dentists. Most of us need plumbers, carpenters, and electricians. We need others to work and socialize with, and to help us learn and grow in healthy ways.

Independence doesn't mean we can never depend on anyone else for anything. It means taking care of ourselves. And taking care of ourselves means accepting the help we need from others.

I take care of myself and accept what I need from others.

Decisions

We may have stopped allowing others to control us, but still feel unsure about making independent choices. It takes practice to gain confidence in this area.

We can clarify the issues and options we face by organizing all the information we have. When we are trying to decide whether or not to do something, it may help to list all the pros and cons we can think of.

Examining the possible negative consequences of our actions doesn't have to immobilize us with fear. In fact, viewing our actions more realistically can be reassuring.

Eventually, we just have to make the best decision we can. With our Higher Power's help, we will grow better at making good decisions. In the meantime, we can just do our best and be patient with ourselves.

With God's help, I can make my own decisions.

Well-Being

We have been working at finding well-being all along our pathway. But we may be uncertain about exactly how to define well-being. We may use words like *happiness, peace,* or *serenity.* But what do these words really mean?

We may try many ways to find happiness unsuccessfully. We may pursue a career, acquire material comforts, perhaps even wealth or prestige, and still not feel happy. We may have many different experiences and relationships, and still not find happiness.

Our well-being—or the lack of it—lies solely within us. No external achievement can put this quality in our lives. It grows out of accepting the things we cannot change and taking responsibility for ourselves. It comes out of spiritual growth and development. It works from the inside out, not the other way around.

I can find the source of my well-being within myself.

Joyfulness

Joy is always found in the present moment. When we focus fully on whatever we're doing, here and now, we can experience the joy of letting go of the past and the future.

We may have been worried or upset, but when we turn our attention to the present moment, we discover that we are just fine. All the pain and worry were only in our minds. Actually, we may be quite comfortable, feeling well, and perhaps even enjoying a meal, music, television, reading, or the company of others.

We may miss a great deal of joy because we expect it to be unusual, dramatic, and spectacular. We are waiting for lights to flash and bells to ring. But the truth is that joy is here, right now, waiting for us to notice it. Chances are, in this very moment, we are just fine.

I find joy in the present moment.

Self-Care

We are responsible for taking care of ourselves every day of our lives, remembering all aspects of our well-being: physical, mental, emotional, and spiritual.

We can take care of ourselves physically by eating properly, exercising, resting, and seeing our doctor and dentist regularly. We can take care of our mental selves by reading, learning new things, and giving up false beliefs and magical thinking.

Emotionally, we can take care of ourselves by understanding and accepting our feelings, and finding appropriate ways to express them. We can take care of our spiritual selves through prayer and meditation—our conscious contact with our Higher Power.

I now take care of myself in every way.

Day by Day

There is only one way life can be lived: day by day, hour by hour, and minute by minute. Outside of science fiction, there is no way to travel backward or to skip forward in time.

This arrangement is a very good one. Today is plenty for us to handle. If we concentrate on the decisions and responsibilities of this day, we can cope with whatever comes our way. But if our minds are full of regret over the past and worry about the future, we are too overwhelmed to deal with the present.

We all think about the future, making plans and looking forward to events. But when we waste time and energy in useless worrying, we miss all the opportunities today offers. The best way to create wonderful tomorrows is to live fully, one day at a time.

Day by day, I move forward along the pathway of my life.

Possibilities

If a small acorn looked up from the ground at a giant old oak tree, thinking, *I can never make one of those,* it probably wouldn't. Look at any seed: apple, tomato, pumpkin, maple, marigold, or sweet pea. Is there any sign from the appearance of these tiny seeds to indicate the tall trees, lush foliage, or abundance of fruits and vegetables they bring?

We may sometimes doubt our own ability to accomplish our goals. We may still see ourselves in the shadow of past experiences. But seeds don't develop best in shadows. They need sunlight, water, and good, nutritious soil.

We can nurture ourselves and bring forth a magnificent harvest, grow tall and strong and withstand the ever-changing seasons of life. We can replace the shadow with the light of faith and hope. We can remember the acorn.

I am open to all the wonderful possibilities within myself and God's universe.

This Too Shall Pass

As we move along the pathways of our lives, we pass through many experiences and feelings. Some of them are joyous and seem all too brief. Others may be painful and seem never-ending. But nothing in this world truly lasts forever.

Every experience has a purpose, and when that purpose has been served, the experience passes. Faith in our Higher Power can help us to believe this. It can also help to remember other times when we felt bad, and it did, indeed, pass with time. If we seem to be experiencing the same kind of pain and loss over and over, we may need to make some changes in our attitudes and behaviors.

Life is change. Progress travels up and down a winding road. Whatever difficulties we have today, this too shall pass.

I will remember that nothing lasts forever, and I have as much to learn from the pain as the joy.

Centeredness

Being centered means remembering who and what we are all the time. It means keeping our spiritual core in charge. It means being fully in the present.

Centeredness keeps us from wasting our thoughts on the past or the future. When we remain centered, we cannot be tossed about by the whims, attitudes, or actions of others. We can't lose ourselves in other people's feelings or problems.

If we feel our centeredness slip away from us, we can always get it back. Meditation can be very helpful in this. We can close our eyes and imagine a dark cloud within us. Now we go into the cloud, toward its center. When we get to the center, we will be in a very bright light and the cloud will disappear, like fog burning off in the sunshine. In this bright light, we are completely peaceful and happy, and can feel the loving presence of our Higher Power.

Remember that we always carry this center around with us wherever we go.

I remain focused on my spiritual center.

Starting Over

We may now feel as if we're embarking on a whole new life. We're developing completely different ways of thinking and behaving. The outer circumstances of our lives may appear to be changing for the better.

This is a very exciting and wonderful time, but it can also be confusing and scary. At times, we may feel like explorers, charting a new course through the wilderness. Without our old markers of familiar behavior, we may feel lost.

But many others have traveled this way before, and they can help us. We can attend meetings to gain insight and encouragement from others. We can remember to keep in touch with our Higher Power through prayer and meditation.

Starting over doesn't have to be done alone. All the help we need is available to us, if we just ask for it.

I will use the help available to me in working my program.

Saying Yes

We have been learning to stop doing things we don't want to do, but feel compelled to do. We have tried to define some personal boundaries. We have been working on learning to say no.

But recovery from codependent behavior also means learning to say *yes*. We can say yes to health, growth, and spiritual development. We can say yes to fun, happiness, and freedom from being controlled by other people's problems. We can say yes to life and love.

We can take care of ourselves, ask for what we need from others, and accept our own goodness. We can rediscover our talents, abilities, interests, and passions. We can be honest and assertive with others. We can open our eyes to the beauty all around and within us. We can say yes to God and to ourselves.

I am ready to accept all good things into my life.

Affirmations

To *affirm* means to make firm or solidify. Positive statements we repeat to ourselves can help solidify the changes we are making. They can help us to change our thinking and overcome old negative statements.

We can create or select specific affirmations for the problem areas of our lives. If we need to work on our self-esteem, we can use an affirmation like, *I love and feel good about myself,* or *I deserve success, happiness, and good health.* If we need to remember to set goals, take care of our bodies, assert ourselves, or let go of a particular behavior, we can design affirmations to promote those positive changes.

Affirmations can be thought, spoken, sung, listened to on tape, or written down. The more we use affirmations, the more we will believe them and make necessary changes.

I use affirmations daily.

Guilt in Recovery

As we grow healthier and happier, we may sometimes feel a bit guilty. How can we feel so good while others we have been close to still suffer? How can we be good people and leave others behind as we move along?

It is natural to have these thoughts and feelings. We want others to heal and grow as we are. But we don't have to let these feelings hold us back. We can remember our powerlessness over others and their responsibility for themselves. We can enjoy our progress, knowing others must follow their own path.

We can remember that our wellness doesn't cause other people's problems or addictions. Positive changes in us harm no one, and letting ourselves slip backward helps no one. We can keep moving on, wishing the best for others, but knowing their happiness and health are not our responsibility.

My recovery is important and harms no one.

Faith in Ourselves

We may have heard about how a "positive attitude" can change our lives for the better. But trying to be positive may have felt artificial or useless in the face of difficult circumstances.

We can't just wake up one day and decide to have a positive attitude. It must come from our beliefs and self-image. All the changes we have been working on can result in a more positive outlook.

As we learn about ourselves, take responsibility for our lives, and let go of self-defeating behaviors, we grow to believe in ourselves. Experience shows us our true abilities, talents, and skills. Life seems full of the potential for happiness and success as we grow more open to such possibilities. We grow to believe in the goodness of life, our Higher Power, and ourselves.

I have faith in myself, my Higher Power, and my future.

Changes

We began this journey by deciding to make some changes in ourselves and our lives. We struggled through the process of recognizing and letting go of some old patterns of thinking and acting. We learned to accept the changes necessary for our recovery from self-defeating behaviors.

Although we may have come a long way from the beginning of our journey, we may discover that the changes are not over. Our lives, relationships, circumstances, and selves continue to change day by day, year by year, for as long as we live.

We have learned that changes can be positive, promoting our growth, health, and happiness. When we lose a job or business, we may discover another talent or skill in a new line of work we never would have pursued otherwise. When some relationships end, others begin. Old circumstances have to be swept away for new ones to take their place. Each change helps us to learn, grow, and move forward on our journey of life.

I accept change as a continuous part of life.

Simple Pleasures

Our minds are constantly working, processing thousands of bits of information. Lists of things we need to do, decisions we're making, thoughts of people, relationships, events, duties, schedules, and even working our program—all vie for our attention.

Amazingly, we usually manage to accomplish most, if not all, of what we need to do. But all of this busyness may keep us moving so fast that our days slip by before we even notice.

We can fulfill all of our obligations and still take time to find enjoyment in life. If we remember to focus on each present moment, we can discover many small pleasures: beautiful sounds, colors, smells, and tastes; silence; warmth; safety; smiles; hugs; beautiful thoughts and words. These simple pleasures, and many others, provide the joy in life.

I am fully aware of and enjoy all the simple pleasures in my life.

Growth

As children, we may have looked forward to being "all grown up." We may have attached this magical moment to some specific rite, such as getting a driver's license, graduating from school, or getting married.

But experience teaches us that no one ever becomes all grown up. There is no moment in life when the need for further growth suddenly and permanently ends.

At first, this may upset us. We may not want to have to deal with any more stretching, learning, and changing. We may believe it would be much easier if everything would just stay the same forever.

But continuous growth is not a punishment; it's a gift. Each new day is another chance to improve ourselves physically, mentally, emotionally, and spiritually. It's the best blessing we can receive.

I am grateful for the opportunity of continued growth.

A Moment to Reflect
Meditations for Codependents

Letting Go
Setting Boundaries
Accepting Ourselves
Living Our Own Lives